THE 29 RULES FOR CAR FLIPPING SUCCESS!

$127,000   12/12

The inner thinking of a car flipping vet

By Tony Bandalos

ISBN: 9781692360443

PREFACE

The 29 Rules for Car Flipping Success" is meant to be the mindset and thinking behind the art of flipping cars for massive profits. It is in no way intended to be an in-depth step-by-step guide on how to flip cars for profit.

The 29 rules in this book are topics that I think should have importance when playing the car flipping game. My thoughts come from many years of real world experience.
The rules are not in order, I just wrote them as they came to mind. I hope you enjoy it. Please reply to my email and let me know what you liked or disliked about the guide. Thank you!

To your car flipping success!
tony@howtobuyandsellyourcars.com
-Tony

TABLE OF CONTENTS

RULE 1

Keep Searching

*M*any people who get started in the car flipping game don't have enough patience and give up way too quickly. People think just because they are searching for deals, and can't find something quickly, there is no opportunity.

There are many flaws here because what if you simply don't know how to spot the good deals because of lack of market research? Or, because you're looking in the wrong places? And because you simply don't have a trained eye to spot them out?

Through my many years of actually doing this, I will tell you that yes, I've had a week or two with no real deal finding. But just as you persist, one will eventually pop up, and when it does, it will be a good one. If you keep searching for deals, they will appear. All you need is 30 minutes a day while sitting on the couch

.

RULE 2

Market Research, Buyers and Sellers

You live in a specific town and city. The more you know your market, the easier you'll be able to find deals. You may be in a city where trucks are popular and sell fast, or you may live in a town where American cars are the thing.

Learn your market, know the market pricing on specific cars that you plan to flip and when a deal pops up, you'll know if you need to jump on it quick, or end up missing out on the deal. It's also important to know what type of person you are selling too and who you are buying from. You always want to cover your ass and be careful. If a buyer seems fishy on the phone, or in person, try and get out of the situation fast.

Always meet in public places when selling a vehicle like shopping centers or a populated area. If you feel uncomfortable, bring a friend when looking at or when you are selling a car.

Most times all will be fine because you'll be able to weed them out from the phone/texting stage that I cover in my un-cut guide on flipping cars for massive profits.

I can tell you this because I have real world experience selling many cars through my 20 plus years of doing this. Like I said, I sold my first car when I was 15 years old in a Safeway parking lot for my stepfather all alone. If I can do this at 15, you can do this now.

The same goes when looking at a car that you are planning to purchase, most times this goes very smooth. If you feel uncomfortable about going to the seller home to view a vehicle, just meet up in a well light area in public.

Most times it's a great sign if a seller invites you to their home to view the car. This shows that they have nothing to hide. But it's also ok if they decide to meet you in public places, because they, like you are just trying to protect their butt. I've sold many cars right outside my mother's house.

RULE 3

Getting Over Missed Opportunity

*T*here will be times where you think you have a super deal on your hands… but things end up happening, and you end up missing out because another buyer was swift to act and close. Get over it quick and just move on.

Many times when this happens to me, I end up finding a better deal anyway. Just know that, there will ALWAYS be deals out there. You just need to stay persistent and know how to spot them. Yes you may lose some time because you went out to look at the deal, or deals, but it's just part of the game. The more you look at and deal with, the more you'll get. It only takes one car for you to bank $2,000 or more.

RULE 4

Be First!

*M*ost times it's advantageous to be the first one looking at a potential deal. Why? Because you have a better shot at making and closing the deal fast.

Most times this work's best when the seller is motivated to sell. This is what I call the first mover advantage. Immediately after you find a deal and ensure it passes your inspection, make an offer (most times in cash) and try to close the deal fast.

On the other hand, not being first can also work to your advantage because of the seller finally learning that their initial asking price was way too high and now deciding that they really want to sell and get rid of the car.

This is when you come in with a cash offer, and they are emotionally at the point where they just want to get rid of their ride and are glad to sell you the vehicle so you can take it off their hands. I can easily elaborate through a few pages on this topic from many stories and experiences, but I think you get the point. If you want to get more information on this through real stories, follow the F1 Formula program that you've invested in.

RULE 5

Cash Talks!

*y*ou know this! We all know this, even in this day and age, cash still talks. Believe me, I'm a big fan of digital money and crypto currency, but we're still not at the point where we can negotiate in Bitcoin, but I can't wait.

Always bring cash, or at least enough for a deposit when taking a look at a potential deal. This shows the seller that you are serious and it will also give you an upper hand when negotiating. I always bring enough cash with me to close and walk away with any car deal I'm looking at. There are many ways you can negotiate when you have cash including bringing a friend that you supply with some of your cash.

So when in the heat of the moment, you can show as if you are really asking your friend for some extra cash to get the deal.

RULE 6

Always Point Out Flaws

This is key in negotiation because if you know your stuff, you'll always get a better deal. This shows the seller that you know what you're looking at. Better yet, if you know how much it will cost to make those repairs, you can work it right into your offer on the spot.

I talk about this in much greater details throughout my in-depth trainings, but you get the point, if the car looks like it needs tires, or a break job, let the seller know that you are aware of this and use it as a negotiating tool to lower your offer.

RULE 7

Be Professional

*N*obody likes working with a jerk. Being likable is a learnable skill and actually pretty easy. Be interested in others, hear what they have to say, and they will have an interest in you! Be a boss, be confident.

When dealing with others, you must show confidence and zig and zag through your conversations. Before actually looking at the vehicle, make sure that you know what you're looking at. When dealing on the spot, valuations, specs and inspections are all done by you while being professional.

RULE 8

Master the Value Add

*Y*ou must know how much to invest in your flips and know when to stop. Many people don't know what to repair, how much to fix up and what to leave alone.

Just remember that the more you put into the car, the less you profit. For instance, you may think the car needs new paint, when the fact is, all you need to do is have the hood and roof repainted and maybe the rest of the car buffed out and detailed.

Just keep in mind that you don't need to fix everything to complete a successful flip or make the most in profit.

Yes the car (your money making flip) may need a set of brakes and a light tune-up, but you may not need to put in a new stereo system, or waste the money on a set new shocks that it doesn't need to get top dollar. Many times I use my spruce-up technique that helps me add hundreds of dollars in extra profit on every car flip that I do. For example on the interior I will usually add a simple set of seat covers (if needed), a steering wheel cover, air freshener... something mild and not to heavy smelling, and a few extra tricks on the body and in engine compartment to add maximum value which will be recouped plus more on the sale.

RULE 9

Know When to Cut Your Losses

I Know this may be hard to swallow, but you'll probably will make a few mistakes. Making mistakes and failing is actually a good thing if you learn from them. I will admit it, I did lose money on two or three deals through my car flipping lifetime and I also broke even a few times. But as long as you learn the important lessons throughout your experiences, I think it's totally worth it. For me, I learned that you can't and shouldn't fix everything on a car because you'll end up digging into your profits pretty quickly and it may not be worth the value add. Know when to stop investing. Invest in only what will get you the biggest turns. I also learned how to properly negotiate and buy cars that have the biggest potential in returns with the less amount of work. You need to do the same.

Good thing for you, I cover many of the pit falls that you could easily avoid by following my F1 Formula course. Please login and follow the system. Over the years I've basically mastered what cars to buy, and at what price range to sell at. Cars that need the least amount of work with the biggest return in profit. In the past, I thought that I needed to buy cars that needed a lot of work to make a profit. This cost me a lot of time.

This is not true, there are many cars that you can flip that need nothing but a good detail, maybe a set of new tires, or a light tune-up that allow you to make thousands in profit.

RULE 10

Enjoy What You Do

*B*y no means are these rules set in specific order, but this rule actually should be first. You must enjoy working with automobiles, searching for deals and like doing this to succeed. For me, finding a car deal is fun and making profits from a car flip is pretty damn rewarding. It's always a plus if what you do doesn't feel like work, and you do it because you enjoy what you do.

RULE 11

The Scammer

*T*here will always be a scam. I can't tell you how many times I've been scammed through uncorrelated business ventures and investments, but it's your sole duty to be wise and learn from your experiences. There is a saying that I'm sure you've probably heard of "Fool me once, shame on you… Fool me twice, shame on me" Not sure who wrote it, but it's true. Learn from your mistakes and failures and you'll be alright. If a deal seems too good to be true, there is a good possibility that it is.

If you see a $24,000 car selling for $7,000, red flag. It could be a scam. Be careful on Craigslist, eBay, Facebook, and through other automotive Apps that are commonly used.

The more experience that you have about the going prices for cars in your local area, the quicker you'll be able to tell a good deal from a bad deal, and you'll also be able to spot the scams very easily.

The deals that look too good to be true usually are a common scam normally comes to you by email with a story that they can't or don't have time to see your vehicle, but they will pay you full price and have a transportation company come and pick up the car. They say they'll pay you by PayPal for full asking price, sometimes even more. This is when they start to ask for your personal information like your full name, address, PayPal information, red flag.

Just know that any serious person would not do this. 95% of the time you'd have a viewing, or at least have a phone conversation with the buyer if they are buying sight unseen.

RULE 12

Rolling and Stacking the Dough

*T*his is true especially if you're just getting started. If you stick to your guns and save half of your profit on every car flip that you do, you'll end up with a nice chunk of cash to reinvest into new deals. If you tend to be more aggressive and don't need to use some your profit for daily living... simply roll it all back into flipping more cars for profit. Boom. This is when it really gets fun because you can follow my step-by-step guide on "How-To Turn $1,000 into $10,000 In Profit" from 4-5 car flips.

RULE 13

Private Party, Auction, Or Wholesale

*T*his rule can be a book all on its own, but I want to keep it short and simple for you.

If you're a beginner, I recommend that you start in the **Private Party** market because if you know what you're doing, you can get really good deals. In other words, fish in the private market, buy cars from every day people like you and I who advertise through for sale signs on roads, in online classifieds like Craigslist, newspapers and in penny savers.

Till this day, I still get some of my best deals in the PP market. Why shop here? Well, when buying in the PP market you have an easier time in negotiating and inspecting. Plus at times you'll come across people who simply have no idea what their car is worth and sell it way under value.

Wholesale: I would step up to wholesaling after you learn the PP market. Go out and make a few connections with automotive wholesalers, it's easy because they all want your business. They basically get deals from their own sources of dealers and auctions, and are happy selling them to you for a few hundred above cost for a quick profit. This is their business model. They sell a lot of cars at lower margins. Then you go out and retail the cars. There are pro's and con's to this method, but is still a great way to get profitable deals. I cover this method extensively through my video course as well.

Auction cars: I would use this method if you are starting to feel really comfortable at analyzing deals and know how to turn great profits. Auctions are tricky because you are not alone here. You are competing against at least 25-50 bidders at a time because of the online bidding systems.

Remember, you are also bidding against people that you can't even see! Auctions are cut-throat nowadays and it's my last place to fish for deals. You can get wrapped up emotionally during the bidding process and if you don't know the market and your numbers, you could lose your shirt really really fast on a bad deal.

Just know that you must have experience when playing the auction game. You can carve a niche and play with salvage automobiles, but that's another playbook that I cover in my in-depth courses. In conclusion, if you're a newbie and want to succeed with the odds in your favor, follow my step-by-step method and start flipping in the PP market. You'll do great there, I guarantee it.

RULE 14

The Savvy Negotiator

*K*nowing how to properly negotiate is key to financial success. Have you ever heard the term "You make the money on the buy, and not on the sale"? It's a popular real estate phrase because the fact is, if you get a good deal on the buy, you will always make money. It's kind of like already having money in the bank. An asset just waiting to be cashed out.

If you have a good deal, you will always make a sale. Another saying is "You don't get what you deserve, you get what you negotiate". Learn to negotiate win-win deals when buying, and when selling.

The more you practice this, the better you'll get. There are many proven negotiating strategies that I've learned and used over the years that are essential to use if you want to add hundreds and even thousands of dollars in profit to your bottom line. One of my favorites is the **Made Up Competitor** negotiation strategy if you don't have any other real cars that you are looking at. You can use this from both ends of the coin, when selling, or when buying a vehicle. Essentially, I like to use this strategy when buying a vehicle…

To act as if I am looking at another similar car that has more mileage but is in better condition and selling for less money. You simply make up the terms to get a better deal on your end. It's simply negotiating power.

RULE 15

Capital and Securing Funds

*L*ook, when getting in this game, you need some start-up cash. Many people who contact me say they have no money to play the game. My answer, get some, then come back and ask my advice.

10 years ago I used to say if you have $500 in seed capital, you could get a deal and get started but it will most likely be a beater car. With that said, you could fairly double or even 3X that amount on a single car flip that should always be your goal. To at least make a 100% return on your investment. But it's ok if you start out and can only make a 30%-50% return. The higher your play

money budget the easier it will be to make better profits. To me the sweet spot is in the $3-9k range in selling prices.

Now days, I say don't even bother if you can't afford to play with at least $1,000 in starting seed capital. You need to remember, this is an investment. You will not lose this money. The goal is to double, and if you do good, 2.5X or 3X your money on every car flip that you complete.

The more cash you have to play with, the better deals you'll be able to get and the quicker you can multiply your cash. I cover this in great detail within my car flipping programs and also show you what cars to get, and how much you should be investing for maximum profits.

Taking out cash from a credit card: Do it if you can. If you can take out $2,000 - $3,000 from your card at the beginning of your billing statement, and use that cash to flip a car within 2-3 weeks, then pay it back in full, then consider yourself way ahead of the game. You just took advantage of free money besides some of the transfer fees for using cash advances. Not too shabby. I've had quite a few of my students follow my advice on this and really pulled themselves out of a hole. If you do this, be sure that you have proper knowledge and know how to get good deals and are confident before borrowing money.

Just imagine taking out $2,500 from a cash advance on your credit card. You take out that money, you find a deal for $2,000.00 maybe a 2007 Toyota Camry for instance… you put in $250.00 for a few fixes. You're in the car for $2,250.00. You put an ad out for $4,800 because it has good mileage, roughly 88,000 miles. You flip it quick for $4,500.00. That's a quick 2,250.00 in profit.

Congratulations, you've just doubled your money! This type of thing can happen every single day. You just need to know how to spot the deals. You pay back your card, now you have your own cash to do the same thing over and over. You may think no way, but this is the kind of thing that's consistently put five figures in monthly profit in a lot of people's pockets.

Borrowing money from a relative: If you have good trusting relationships with friends and family, then why not borrow? I had a young kid, one of my students borrow $1,500 from his step father to flip a truck. He ended up paying his stepfather back the $1,500 including $200 as a thank you, and he still made a $2,000 profit on his first flip after following my advice. Not too shabby if you ask me.

Sooner or later if you want to move up in life and actually get somewhere, you need to make a move. You need to get off your ass and take action. Getting advice and reading my books and taking my courses are great for you. But you need to make the moves.

Stop being fearful and just go out and get it. If you fail, who cares? We all fail. Just pick yourself back up, pick up the ball and keep playing. Success only comes after participation in the game.

RULE 16

Abide By Or Break The Rules?

*T*his is a fun one. Did you know most successful people in life never really followed the rules? It's true, go ahead and do some research. Many successful people like Mark Cuban, Jay-Z, Nikola Tesla, Thomas Edison, Henry Ford, Andrew Carnegie, Steve Jobs, and Bill Gates never really followed the rules.

There is a reason why we are threatened everyday by rules and laws. They don't want us on top. They want to keep us down. They are the very ones who never follow the rules, even the rules they make for us. I don't want to get into rant full of dirty details (which should be another book). The system is rigged, but we still have a way out if we look for a way, but here's the deal…

I get questions every day... people saying "But Tony, I can only flip so many cars per year in my state....what can I do?" Ohh Tony, is this legal?" Ohh Tony, I really want to do this but I'm afraid that if I flip too many cars they will come and get me..."

Listen, if you are one of these people who is too afraid to buy a car and sell it, then maybe this is not for you. It will just give the people who have the guts and common sense more deals to profit from.

There are guys out there every day who flip cars. I do cover strategies throughout my in-depth courses about how to flip 5-8 cars per year legally, and how to legally flip 4X that amount if you want to. There you go. There is an option, but I can't mention it here. It's too much for the 29 rules. Stop worrying about the small details. Find a deal, make some money, then see where you want to go. There is one thing that I know for sure.

THERE IS NO LAW stating how many cars you can own. Jay Leno has over 280 cars in his car collection.

He keeps buying more, and I believe he sells some. So what if you bought a car, drove it for two weeks and decided to sell it because you just didn't like it anymore? So what? What's the big deal? Just go out and get a deal! I think most people never get started because of having too much fear. It's a little pathetic to me, nobody will ever get anywhere hung up in fear. Remember NIKE? "Just Do It!" Just as I do, sometimes it's better to ask for forgiveness later, than to first ask for permission. Beware! I am in no way promoting illegal advice, I am only asking you to smell the coffee! 17 year old kids are making a fortune. Will you have known and still know of many car flippers who buy and sell cars all month long. Most of them get and work with open titles. Some of them register 20-40 cars per year under their name without any issues and have been doing so for many many years. Take one step at a time. Find a deal, make a deal, profit off of a deal, celebrate your profitable deal, and then see what's next in your adventure of car flipping.

RULE 17

Using OPE

O PE stands for **other people's experience**. This is something that I've applied all of my life and what it comes down to is simply learning from others who are successful and have the experience. Model them, copy them and emulate.

Don't take advice from people who have no business giving advice. There are many people who have just opinions, we all do, and most of our opinions should be kept to ourselves unless asked upon, or unless we know that we can help somebody learn something or see a specific point of view

Opinions that come from experts, people with direct experience, and a deep knowledge of a particular topic that you are interested in should be listened to and considered very carefully.

Just remember when getting advice from others, ask yourself "is this person qualified to talk to me on this specific topic?" Seek knowledge from the people who's been there and done it. Don't listen to every Joe Schmo on the street about what they think about any topic unless you know that they have some type of qualification.

RULE 18

Celebrating Victories

*T*his is important and I will say that I'm guilty of not always doing this myself. If you're here still reading this guide then you, like me, are a go getter. Congrats, welcome to the go-getter club. Let's get um. A lot of times we are too hard on ourselves. We don't give ourselves enough credit. We need to make sure that we stop and smell the roses, especially when we are victorious. So if you completed a profitable flip, or even if you think you failed because you only made $200, or $300 or almost broke even... you still need to remember to celebrate it.

Most importantly because you actually did something, you made something happen, and that's a good thing. You're on the right track, even if it's as small as acknowledging it to yourself tapping your own shoulder and talking to yourself. It works. So after your next profitable car flip, celebrate your new beginning in creating extra income for yourself and for your family. It's a real skill-set that once you learn, nobody can ever take away from you.

RULE 19

Using Brains or Trains

*T*his is a good one. My father always said "common sense isn't so common". I mean, it's funny if you think about it, but it's true.

In business and in life in general, you need to think on your toes, and it also helps if you're a sharp and quick thinker. I get it, for some people, they just can't do what we do. And that's ok. They can keep their jobs working minimum wage making $12hr at Ross or McDonald's. I'd rather take a weekend, flip a car and pocket 2-3k. But in reality, all of it is a learnable skill, even being sharp.

Just like a knife, you need to sharpen your skills and sharpen your brain. When you don't use a limb it will atrophy. The same with your brain. If you don't use it, you'll lose it. So how do you train yourself to use your brains rather than your trains? Simple. Never stop learning. I can't tell you how much I love to read and write, and over a variety of topics I might add. I love investing, I love stocks, I love travel, I love personal development, and I love listening to motivational speeches from my heavy hitter dudes like the Rock, Stallone, and Arnold, all of those guys.

These are my OG heavy hitter success buddies. I follow their lead for inspiration when I need it because the fact is, we all need it. Stay sharp, and get smart, but action still trumps smarts any day.

Ask any successful person out there... What is more correlated to success? Being smart and having a high IQ, or simply having the courage and guts to take massive action? They will tell you, it's all about taking action, getting out there, and doing something!!!

Learn and make the moves.

RULE 20

Making the Deal Come to You

*D*on't look too anxious when buying or selling. You need to play your poker face at all times. If you look too excited when looking at a deal, the seller will spot you out with a quickness. People are not stupid. You need to maintain your bluff and act as if it's not that great of a deal even if it is.

The same is true when selling your vehicle. Don't jump on the first cash offer that you get on the spot, or even look too excited when you get an offer that's more than what you expected, or even at the exact price point that you expected.

Looking too excited, or accepting the offer too quickly makes the deal look bad. It makes the buyer think "wow, he accepted the deal so quick ....I wonder if something is wrong with it, or if I probably could have gotten it much cheaper?" This can change the buyers mind pretty quickly and you could possibly lose the deal from the buyer trying to back out.

Usually when I get an offer in person, I hold a 10-15 second pause and don't look too excited at first. Then I usually come up with a 'meet me half way' offer and negotiate an additional $200 or $300 from their offer price just to play the game. This is when you know a deal will be made and you're selling the car.

I also cover the bounce back method within the F1 training and how you can get sellers calling you back to close on your initial offer, and you end up getting the deal cheaper and save hundreds more off your initial offering price.

RULE 21

Ad-Vantage

*K*nowing how and where to advertise your deals are crucial to your success. Just know that there are proven ways to word your ads and list your vehicles for sale. Verbiage, terminology, listing points are important as well as the style of photos used. Videos are a huge plus now days. Use all ways to advertise and you'll see your cars move out the door pretty quickly.

Example: In your ads, you always want to list the benefits of your deal and expand upon them. If your vehicle has low mileage, you better be sure to flaunt it in your ad.

"2012 Honda Accord ONLY 65k Miles! Excellent Condition, Cold AC, One Owner Car, New Tires!"

I always like to list recent fixes and value that has been added to the car with a price point. Like if you put new tires on the vehicle, in the ad I would also have a bullet that said:

✓ New tires all around! Just had new tires installed balanced and mounted last month, cost $648.67
✓ New oil change and air cleaner, cost $115.00
✓ More benefits…
✓ More benefits…

Also insert at least 6-10 great pictures of the vehicle with nice backgrounds. The backdrop of your photo is VERY important whether you realize it or not. You always want to take pictures of your vehicle with it sitting in a good location with trees, or a clean looking nice neighborhood background.

You don't want to take your photo like you just washed it in a parking lot with other cars that make it look like a car lot, or with the parking floor that looks like it has oil leaks all over stained the cement. Pay attention to the details, it pays off!

Then I would list your car at the KBB Retail price of $8,570.00. Then list your asking price of only $6,900.00 or best offer!

Call: 555-555-5555

In fact, I have a whole video module covering this topic and how you can use it to your unfair advantage by selling almost anything at retail or a little below retail pricing. <u>Login to your members area here and apply these methods now</u>!

Of course, having a good deal is a big part of selling something fast. If you don't have a good deal, it will be hard to sell anything. There needs to be good value at good pricing.

RULE 22

Title, Documents and Bill Of Sale

*K*eeping good records of your deals are important, especially when starting out. I give all of my students a templated document that allows them to fill out simple math numbers. Price of car, repairs, paperwork cost, insurance etc. This allows you to see what your total investment is and how much you can expect to profit.

As you get better at flipping, you may get lazy and try to keep track of rough numbers in your head. That's ok. But it's always good to see exactly what you have invested and how much you are expecting to make back.

After agreeing on a price and getting paid, you'll want to start preparing your documents (or even have them ready before the sale). You basically have the title for the vehicle and you'll want to create a BOS to cover your behind.

Bill of Sale - I normally use my BOS template on every car purchase and sale that I make just to cover my butt. Plus it's good record keeping.

What should it say or cover? I normally have the selling price, the VIN number, license plate number (if attached to the car), and a brief description of the vehicle being sold or acquired. Of course include your name and the other parties' information which should be signed and dated. This has nothing to do with the title or registration. It's just a separate document for your personal records.

You can pretty much have any term or agreement you wish to have on a bill of sale. You could also use it as a contract for a down payment and balance to be collected written with terms. "No refund on deposit if balance not paid within 30 days" etc. I have done this and have executed on that term when selling a sail boat in Hawaii. I had a bill of sale on my boat, the buyer put a down payment of $3,000 and said he would pay me the balance of $5,500 in 30 days. I gave him up to 60 days, he never dellvered. I executed the contract and kept the $2,500. I then sold it to another buyer who had the full amount in cash within 2 weeks.

Yes it costed me an additional $250 in the boat slip rental but I ended up making out and ended up getting much more than my asking price. This is the game. Did I feel bad? No. It was a contract, plus I also gave him an additional 30 days but he never came up with the cash.

It's funny because he asked me if he could sail the boat to Maui many times before he paid it off. I think he was planning to steal it from me, but I never gave him the papers.

The title: Leaving the title open. Many people in the car flipping game try to acquire open titles when getting a deal. An open title means that when the vehicle is transferred from seller to buyer, the title is not immediately filled out by the buyer. The title is open.

This allows the buyer to buy the car and sell it to another party without being seen or involved in the transaction through a title transfer at the DMV. This allows the seller or the middle man to avoid paying taxes and fees for registration. Using an open title method can save you a lot of money.

This is illegal in many states because in reality the motor vehicle wants to get paid every time a car is sold through transfer fees and taxes. I do not recommend that you do this, but I do know of many people who do this year in and year out. If you find good deals, paying the extra for tax and fees should not make a big difference in your profit margin anyway.

I have registered many cars in my name over the years and have flipped them for great profits. This rule can get pretty lengthily so I will cut it short here hoping that you get the idea.

RULE 23

Confident Action = Positive Results

*y*ou must rid your fears and take action to succeed. You can also turn your fear into courage. It happened to me when I leaped off a 60 foot cliff into a cenote while in Mexico on one of my world trips.

When I was at the bottom looking up at people jumping off, it really didn't seem that high or too bad. But when I got up there on the rock and looked down over the ledge, I did get scared. I had fear of jumping, but in that moment, I took that fear and turned it into action and just leaped off.

It happened so quickly, and before I knew it I was swimming back up to the surface for some air. That intense drop into the deep cold water really gave me a sense of power and I felt great! Enough to do it again. I conquered my fear. It felt really good. Most times when you are scared shitless, you just need to take that leap of faith.

Many people overthink every situation. I think we need to be like kids more often. Kids see the world simple. We as adults overcomplicate things because we have more education or brainwashing, whatever you want to call it. Seriously, there is some truth to the quote "Ignorance is bliss".

If you want to get into the game of car flipping, or buying and selling cars for profit, whatever you decide to call it, then make it your sole goal to succeed and commit to it.

Don't let the fear of getting a bad deal, or not knowing what to do next stop you. The fact that you are here reading this guide already sets you apart, and I believe just from the information in this book you have more than enough to get started.

Learn the essentials, but don't study too much. There needs to be a point where you just jump in. Take action! Get a deal, then take your next step. Hopefully you won't have to worry about getting a bad deal because you'll be following my advice on how to get good deals.

There is no need researching this topic for months before you get started. Just follow my F1 Formula system and get started today!

RULE 24

The 3 Major Automotive Compartments

*M*y father taught me this and it does makes sense. Especially when buying cars at auctions.

Whenever looking at a vehicle, you need to look at it and divide it into three separate sections. Please note that I cover this extensively in the **F1 Formula car flipping program that you should have access to if you've upgraded to the F1 VIP course**.

1: The body and frame.

2: The engine, electrical and suspension.

3: The interior/electrical.

If two of the three major three compartments are good and only one of them needs some kind of work and the deal makes sense, then go for it.

What you don't want to do is get a vehicle that needs paint and body, a timing belt and tune-up, plus some brake work. It's too much major work because you need to work in all three major areas of your vehicle.

What you'd rather be better off doing is to look for a car that only needs some body and paint work … or maybe just an engine swap. Or even less, just a quick detail and oil change.

Stick with this rule for an easier time when flipping cars for profit and you'll be in great shape.

RULE 25

Partners or Running It Solo?

*I*f you like your freedom and like to call your own shots, then run it solo because it isn't hard to do. This business is easy enough to run all by yourself. It's what I do. If you feel that you need a partner for some reason, maybe for financial clout, or simply because you think it'd be fun working with a buddy, then go for it.

Just remember to keep good records of your expenses together and work out a percentage deal. If you agree that you'd both be putting in the same amount of work, or funds, then you basically just split the profit 50/50.

If all your partner wants to be is the money guy, then just pay him a percentage of the loan. So, if he's willing to lend you $5,000 at 10% over 120 days, then that's it. You pay him back $5,500.00 in 120 days. You can create whatever terms you wish as long as the both of you agree on the terms. To me, that's more than enough time to flip many deals. The $500 in interest will be a small fee once you make it happen.

RULE 26

Not Knowing = Blindness

*B*elieve me, I get many emails from people every day telling me they can't find deals. I wish I could help them all but I can't. I do however help all of my **VIP** guys who need my help with this. And yes, even my **VIP** guys need help. Sometimes they come to me saying that they can't find any deals! "Really!" I tell them lol...

We get on a video call, or I'd just reply with a video showing them how to spot a deal in their local city/town, and I do! They say "wow Tony, I've been looking for a week with no success and you get on and in 20 minutes you find a few deals!" Here's the thing. It takes time to train your eye and mind for deals.

You don't know what you don't know. Because I've been doing this for so many years, it's easier for me to spot a deal because as I search for deals, I immediately see the deal, not only the numbers point of view, but from also the value add (the possibilities). It's the same with real estate. If you really look, there is money all over the place just waiting to be picked up. You need to train yourself to spot the deals.

RULE 27

Buying Sight Unseen

*B*elieve it or not, this is a growing trend. 20 years ago you really didn't have much of this, but with all of the online sites and car delivery services around nowadays, it's getting very popular. I must have bought at least 15 cars off eBay including a few classics sight unseen.

The main thing you want to have done is something called a pre-purchase inspection when buying cars unseen, especially if you're looking to buy a car that's higher in value. There are companies that you can hire and for less than $100. They will inspect the car for you can give you a detailed report. It's very good insurance when you're not able to personally see the vehicle before purchase. This is how I sold a few of my exotic cars to buyers across the country who didn't physically see the vehicle except for some high quality pictures and video.

Go ahead, check out sites like www.carvana.com or www.Vroom.com. They buy and sell cars sight unseen. You can also buy cars from online auctions this way but there is a problem. Even with their reports and car facts, auction cars tend to have issues that are not always reported. Just be extra careful if you are buying auction cars sight unseen.

Make sure that you get the deal low enough so if something unexpected does come up, you are able to cover the cost without really digging into your profit margin.

RULE 28

The Scarcity and Abundance Mindset

I get many people commenting on my videos and blogs online saying "Tony, why do you share this stuff... it will create more competition and only get harder for all of us."

First of all, you need to understand that I need to share this stuff because it's my way of giving back. I can't tell you how many thank you emails I get from people saying that learning this skill was the best thing that ever happened to them and to their family.

I love sharing what I know and if I can make a difference in people's life, even if it's just one person or a family at a time, then it's worth it to me. I just love getting emails and success stories from people that I've helped and I also do the same with every other aspect of my life. I share what I love to do, and what I know hoping that it can inspire somebody and make a difference in their lives. Second of all, if you read any success book, you'll come across people talking about. the scarcity and abundance mindset. If you live your life with an ABUNDANT outlook, you will always get more. The more you give, the more you get.

Just realize that there is more than enough for everyone to get rich. A few people like us making some cash flipping cars will not make a difference in the supply. There will always be supply and demand when it comes to vehicles. We just need to be on top of our game so that we can continue to get ours.

And also, you need to remember, not everyone getting into this or buying my programs actually take action. On scarcity, if you live your life being greedy, and with a scarcity mindset, the world will be very small for you. Yes I agree that a penny saved is a penny earned, but if you think small and save your pennies, I believe that's all you'll ever train yourself to look for.

Rather than that, I chose to look for ways to give more. To earn more and not to cut back on spending. I never say "I can't afford it, or it's too much money" I always try to figure a way how I can get it, or a way I can afford something. With that said, try to be optimistic and start finding ways to think in abundance.

RULE 29

Be Like Water

*I*n conclusion, let me leave you with this. In life you will have many choices and decisions. Some will be hard to make, and some easy. Some you'll need to consult with friends or family for advice. Some decisions will make you tense and leave you feeling unsure and restless.

When you feel like this, take time off and don't make a decision at that instant. Sleep on it, and within a few days, maybe even weeks, you'll find your answer. I always went with my gut feeling when making decisions and I've heard that going with your gut is the right choice because it's your innate sense that's telling you something.

Be like water, relax, and think. Then make your decision and follow through. If you end up realizing at a later time that you made a bad choice, no problem. As long as you learn from your mistakes and keep going, it was probably a mistake that you had to make in order to get to the next level anyway. Just do it. Listen to your gut and "be like water" as Bruce Lee always said.

AUTHOR'S BIOGRAPHY

My name is Tony Bandalos. I was born with ambition from parents with a dream on the beautiful island of Hawaii. I hated school because it was boring. I dropped out of high-school after getting into fights, being non-compliant and skipping too many classes when I was 15. Later, from the wishes of my mother and father, I was shipped to N.Y. to live with my older half-brother who was 32 and had a successful construction business in N.Y. when I was 16.

I worked in construction with my brother and learn everything on how to repair and remodel houses while going to night school to get my GED. I went back to college in Hawaii years later only to drop out again because I didn't want to take the required typing and speech classes to get my college degree. I paid my own way. I opened my own car and body shop at 18, flipped cars, did the auction game and have been in the car game ever since.

I started an online business in 2008 and went on to generate millions online. But I still love cars. Cars are my passion and I still enjoy getting deals and flipping for profit. Even to make a $5,000 profit. My latest flip was a Lamborghini Gallardo which put a healthy profit in my pocket.

I believe you can do anything that you put your mind too. If all this book did was inspire you, then I think I did my job. But what would be a greater compliment to me was that if you actually took some of this information and did something with it. Inspiration is good, but applied inspiration is even better. In fact, that's what it's all about.

Go ahead, get out there, find a deal, swallow your fears and transform them into the fuel that you can use to break-through into a new you. A new you that takes massive action. It's never too late to change. To become somebody we never was, we need to do something we've never done.

I hope you enjoyed this short read, I am in no way a professional writer. You may find some grammatical and or spelling errors, and a reason to be nit-picky at me and my work. But before you do, ask yourself, "what have I done lately?"

My goal here was to give you a guide, and some rules that can help you become successful at this "car flipping game". It's not hard, it's simple. Just follow what others have done and you'll go great! If you want to learn more about how to really supercharge your success with car flipping like many of my students have and you don't have access to F1 VIP, check out my other in-depth books and video courses on flipping cars for massive profits here.

If you got this book as a bonus for investing in my other paid programs I also hope you got a golden nugget or two out of it. If you bought this book on Amazon or from my site, then I really thank you for the support. Please reach out if you need extra help in getting to the next level with flipping cars for profit. My team and I are standing by for you.

P.S. Please reply back to this email and let me know how you liked this rule book. I appreciate your feedback and I hope you got something out of it!

Make things happen!

-Tony Bandalos
tony@howtobuyandsellyourcars.com

www.ingramcontent.com/pod-product-compliance
Lightning Source LLC
Chambersburg PA
CBHW021508210526
45463CB00002B/942